TRAIN YOUR BRAIN!

LOGIC GAMES

Illustrations: Anastasiya Tkachova

Text: Alex Howe & Elizabeth Golding

Design: Anton Poitier

This book was conceived, created, and produced by iSeek Ltd.
an imprint of Insight Editions

Insight Editions PO Box 3088 San Rafael, CA 94912

www.insighteditions.com

Library of Congress Cataloging-in-Publication Data available.

ISBN: 978-1-64722-421-9

Manufactured in China

10 9 8 7 6 5 4 3 2

Let's Get Started!

This book is jam-packed with amazing logic puzzles. Some are easy and some are much trickier. Each puzzle has a score, shown by the number on a robot:

See if you can solve each puzzle and give yourself a score to add up when you finish. There is a maximum score of 140. Each time you score points, mark them off on this chart. Mark one gray line with a pencil for each point.

Take your time and do the puzzles in any order you prefer. If you get stuck or want to check your work, the answers are in the back of the book.

Spot the Difference

Three ladybug friends have more spots
than the rest. Can you spot them?

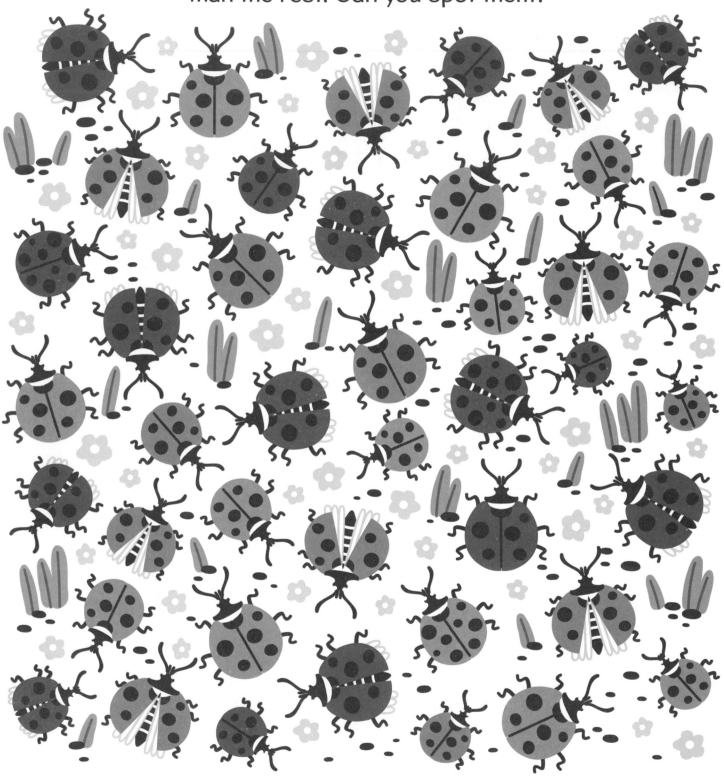

If the three ladybugs had the same number of
spots as all the others, how many spots would
the three friends have all together?

Homeward Bound

Two flocks of birds are flying in opposite directions.
Three birds are lost.

Flock flying east

Lost birds

Flock flying west

Two lost birds join one flock, and the third joins the other flock. The largest flock flies home. Which is it?

Ball Drop

Four animal friends were playing ball in the house.

One of the animals dropped the ball. It bounced from window to window and then landed. Which animal dropped it?

Water Puzzle

An elephant is trying to fill some water tanks.

Which tank will fill up first: A, B, C, D, or E?

Who Lives Where?

Mr. Green, Mrs. White, Ms. Brown, and Mr. Gray live next door to each other. Decide who lives in which house.

House #1

House #2

House #3

House #4

It is a sunny day in Oddtown, but Mr. Green wouldn't know because he is on vacation. Mrs. White has a friend over who brought her dog. Ms. Brown has just painted her front door to match her windows. Mr. Gray likes to watch the wind turn his weather vane.

Mr. Green ☐ Mrs. White ☐ Ms. Brown ☐ Mr. Gray ☐

Puzzling Puzzle

Find the two missing pieces of the puzzle.

Which two pieces will fit? ⬚

Who Went Where?

Three children are going on vacation.
Two of them are going together.

Ellie: I will need flip-flops for the beach, a sleeping bag, and a swimsuit. I won't see the Eiffel Tower, but I will see the Leaning Tower of Pisa.

Ellie

George

Sophia

Things we might take or see:

Sophia: I'm taking a camera and a swimsuit. I'm not going camping. I won't see the Eiffel Tower, but I will see Big Ben.

George: I'm going to Italy. I need a camera, a book, some tickets, and some flip-flops.

Which two children are going on vacation together?

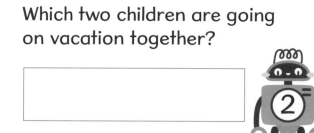

2

Build Bridges!

These islands are connected together by bridges.

There is only one bridge between any two islands. Draw the bridges so that it is possible to walk the shortest distance between any of the islands.

5

Pet Project

Each of these five children has a pet.
Draw a line from each pet to its owner.

Meow!

My pet
hops.

I like my
pet.

My pet purrs.

I do not
have a fish.

I take my pet
for walks.

Zigzag Zebra!

This zebra jigsaw puzzle is missing some pieces.
Can you finish the puzzle?

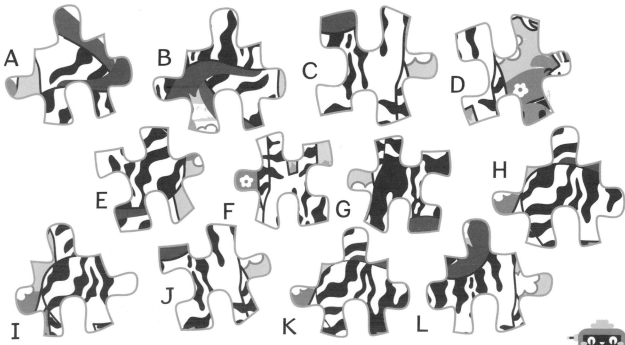

Which two pieces will fit? [ ]

Friend Request

Sam's description of his best friend is missing. Who is Sam's best friend?

My best friend has long, black hair.

Maya

Greg

Rachel

My best friend has red hair.

My best friend is musical.

Jess

My best friend loves to draw.

Claire

Sam

My best friend wears glasses.

Sam's best friend is:

Build a Bot

This machine builds robots with arms and legs, but the creators have forgotten some parts. What are they?

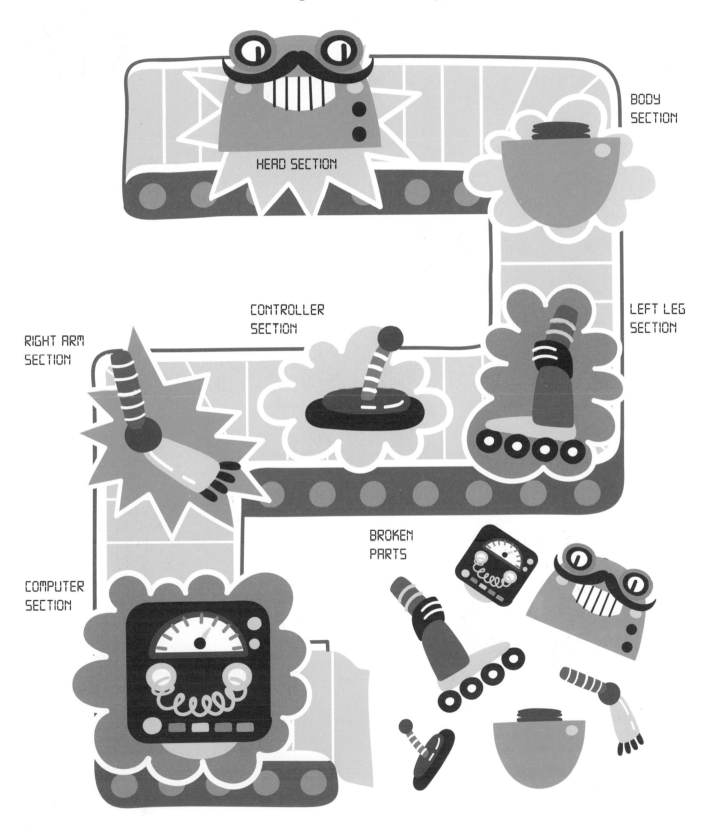

BODY
SECTION

HEAD SECTION

CONTROLLER
SECTION

LEFT LEG
SECTION

RIGHT ARM
SECTION

COMPUTER
SECTION

BROKEN
PARTS

Circle the robot's missing parts.

The Right Shoes

Help these kids pick out their favorite shoes.

I like shoes that make me go super fast.

I want shoes that keep my feet dry.

I like shoes that keep my feet cool.

I hate having to tie laces.

Which shoes were not chosen?

Panda Puzzle

This puzzle is finished, but two pieces in the box came from a different puzzle. Which were they?

The two odd pieces are shown with the correct pieces on the right side of the puzzle. Circle the pieces that don't belong in the puzzle.

Spots and Spikes

One of these groups of dinosaurs has the most spikes on their backs. Does that group also have the most spots?

The friendly dinosaurs

The fierce dinosaurs

The group with the most spikes is:

Does that group have the most spots?

Very Fishy

Some fish are swimming the wrong way. Some fish are much smaller than the others. If the small fish start to swim the right way, how many fish are left swimming the wrong way?

There will be ☐ fish swimming the wrong way.

Castle Confusion

Sir Galahad the knight has come to visit his friend's castle, but he doesn't know which castle it is! He was told it has three turrets, only one entrance, and no windows on the ground floor. Which castle should he visit?

Baron Hardup's castle

Queen Matilda's castle

Prince Frederick's castle

Sir Galahad should visit this castle: [   ]

Cloud Nine

A hot-air balloon has taken off. It needs to reach cloud nine, but it must pass through other clouds to get there. The balloon can go up and move left or right, but cannot go through rain or run into birds. Which clouds will it pass through?

Cloud nine

Circle the clouds the balloon will pass through on the way to cloud nine.

Terrible Twins!

Everyone on this pirate ship is a twin except for the captain! Who is the captain?

Draw a circle around the captain of the ship.

Splish, Splash, Splosh!

Four children are in a messy paint war! Which of them is going to get sploshed and with which color?

George   Ellie   Zac   Sophia

Who gets sploshed with blue paint?

Who gets sploshed with orange paint?

Who gets sploshed with green paint?

Sweet Shuffle

Sort and count the candies by the wrappers.
There were the same number of each to begin
with, but the most popular candy was eaten first.

Draw a circle around the most popular candy.

Pizza Puzzle

Some friends shared four pizzas at their pizza party, but there was some left over.

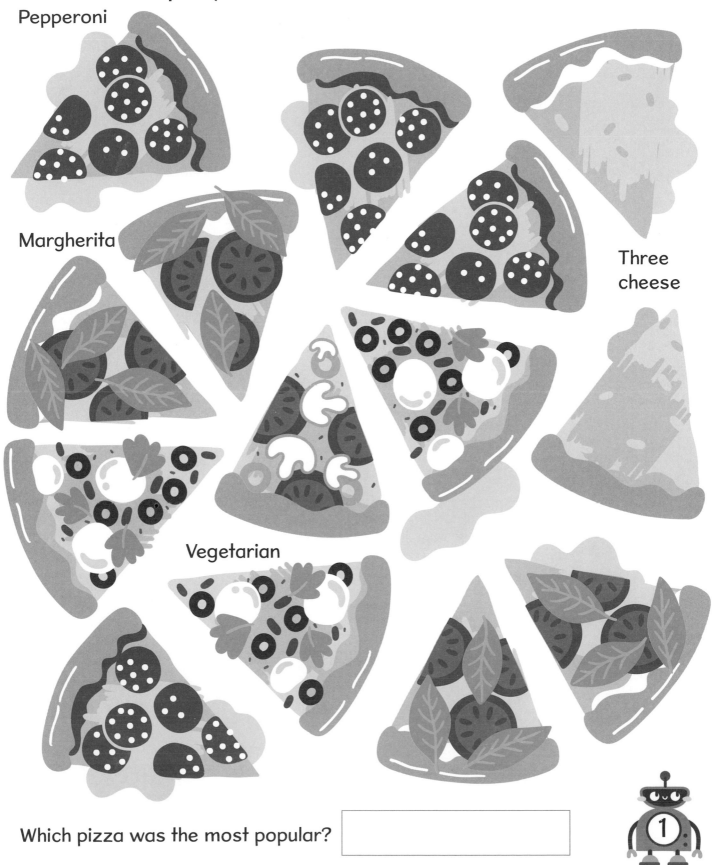

Pepperoni

Margherita

Three cheese

Vegetarian

Which pizza was the most popular? ☐

1

Cake Creator

This machine makes birthday cakes to order.
It begins with a basic cake, then adds items
the customer has ordered.

Start here with
a basic cake.

Candles

Icing

Candles

Sprinkles

Bow

Draw a picture of
the finished cake the
machine made.

Parking Problem

It is Sunday and several vehicles in this parking lot are parked illegally. Read the sign to figure out which vehicle will get a ticket.

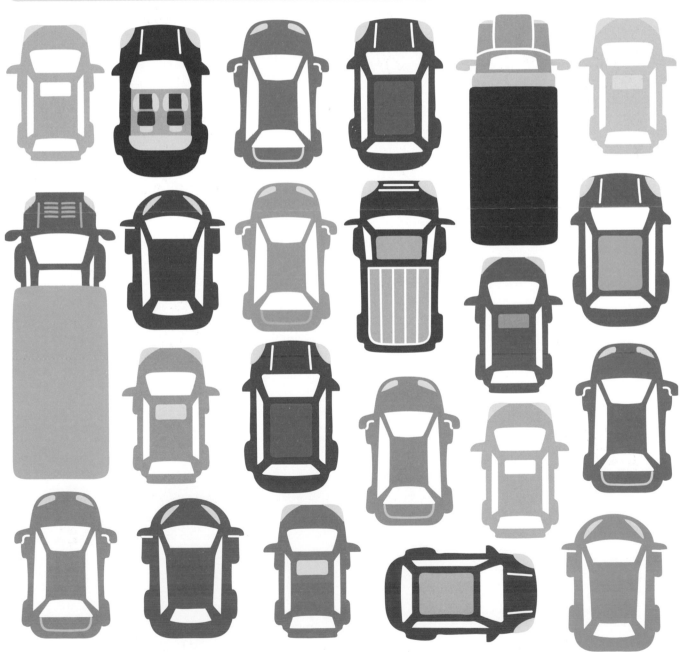

Circle the vehicles that will get a ticket.

Get to School

2 Four friends each get to school using a different mode of transportation. Figure out who uses which method.

Henry

I like it that I get to sit with my friends.

Jamie

I can do jumps on the way to school!

Grace

I just lace up and go!

Stephanie

I can carry my bag in the basket.

Henry [ ]   Jamie [ ]   Grace [ ]   Stephanie [ ]

Which Way?

Ellie and Katie want to hike to the mountains without splitting up. Ellie is afraid of bears, snakes, and water. Katie is scared of foxes, fish, and horses. Which path should they take?

Ellie   Katie   Draw a line on the path they should take.

Ahoy There!

Sailor Sam is looking for his boat in the busy harbor. It has two flags, no anchor, no portholes, a life preserver, and a dog. Which boat belongs to Sam?

Circle Sailor Sam's boat.

All Aboard!

How many people and suitcases will be aboard the train when it arrives at Seatown Station?

Dullswich Station
The train is empty when it arrives. 22 people get on here. 8 people have suitcases.

Funfield Station
3 people get on here and 1 gets off with a suitcase.

Busyville Station
6 people get off here and 2 have suitcases.

Seatown Station
Everyone gets off.

How many people arrive at Seatown Station?

How many suitcases?

Water the Plants

Molly has a watering can and a special funnel system to water her plants. She's made a few mistakes, so some plants won't get watered. Which are they?

A   B   C   D   E   F

These plants will not get watered:

To Tell the Truth

Martha meets a fairy and a unicorn in the forest. The fairy tells fibs every Monday, Tuesday, and Wednesday. She tells the truth on the other days. The unicorn tells fibs on Thursdays, Fridays, and Saturdays. The other days of the week he tells the truth. Look at the picture. What day is it?

Today is:

River Crossing

An old man wants to cross a river and take a fox, a rabbit, and a bag of carrots with him. He has a boat, but it can only fit himself and the fox, the rabbit, or the carrots. If the fox and the rabbit are alone on one side, the fox will eat the rabbit. If the rabbit and the carrots are alone, the rabbit will eat the carrots. How can the man bring the fox, the rabbit, and the carrots across the river without anything being eaten?

Mouse Maze

Take away only three sticks so that the mouse
can get through the maze to eat the cheese.

Cross out the sticks with an X.

Sheep Solution

A farmer has two flocks of sheep and some pens.
He wants each sheep to be alone in each pen.

Move only three fences to make four equal square
pens. Then draw the sheep in their new pens.

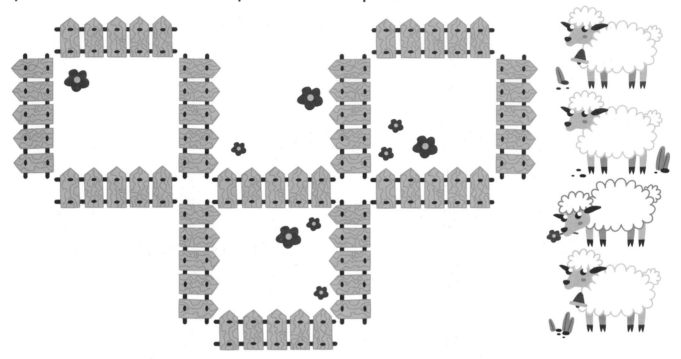

Move only two fences to make five equal square pens.
Then draw the sheep in their new pens.

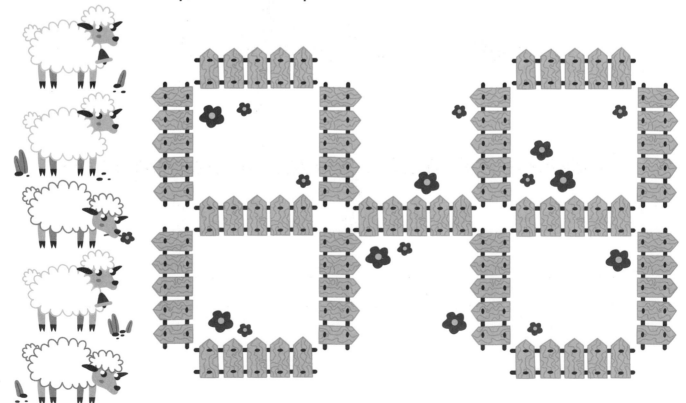

Postal Puzzle

The postal worker is trying to reach a house on the other side of the hedges. Two hedges need to be cut down for her to get there. But which two?

Cross out the hedges with an X.

Matchstick Math

Either remove or move one matchstick in each equation to make the answer correct.

Remove 1 matchstick   6 − 1 = 9

Move 1 matchstick   2 + 5 = 8

Move 1 matchstick   9 − 6 = 7

Move 1 matchstick   4 × 3 = 8

Circle the matches to move or remove.

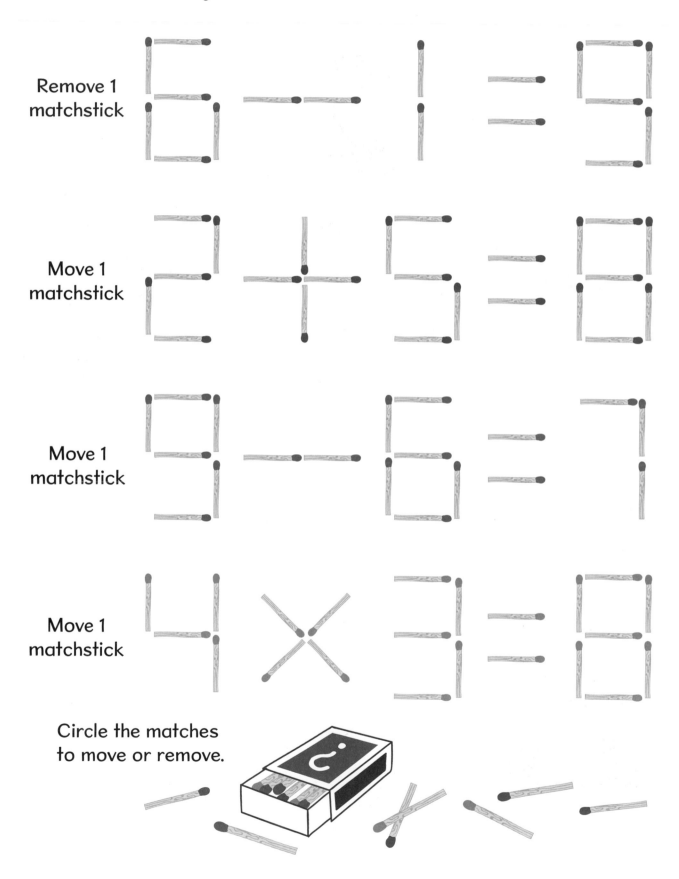

Multiplication Machine

The robots change the numbers from left to right!
Fill in the blanks. The first one has been done for you.

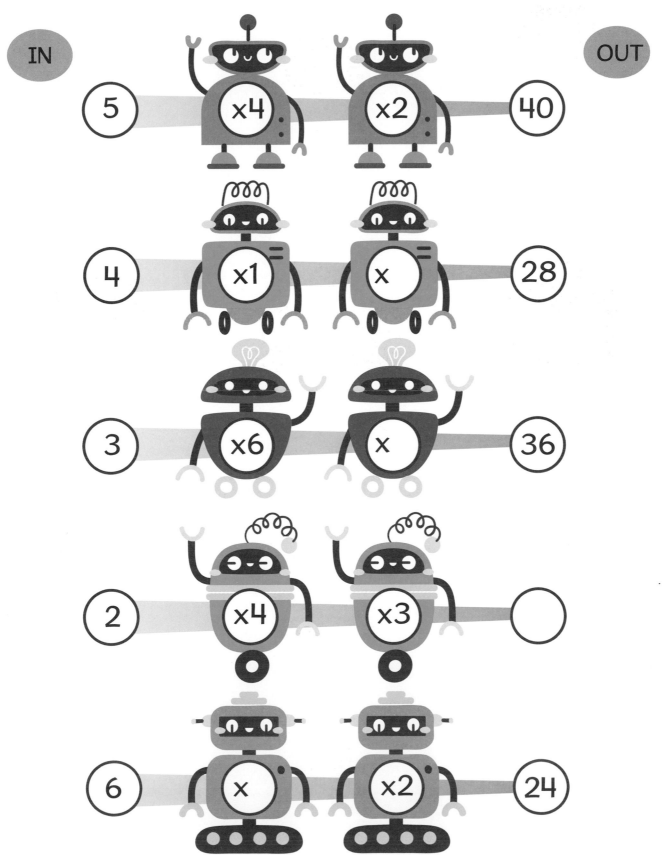

Favorite Food

Four friends are discussing their favorite foods.
Figure out who likes what best.

Jack's favorite is long and thin.

Amy takes the crusts off hers.

Sienna's favorite comes from Italy.

Abeo likes his with peanut butter.

Sophie's favorite is eaten with a spoon.

Harry likes that his usually comes with fries.

Match each person with their favorite food. Write their names in the boxes.

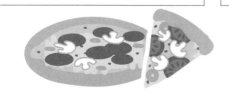

Which Wand?

Calamity the fairy is putting together a new wand
using the Wacky Wand Machine.

Which of these wands is it impossible for her to have made? Circle the answer.

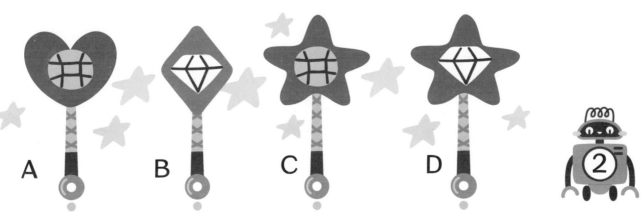

A   B   C   D

Beach Huts

The painter is repainting some of the beach huts, but he wants to make sure there are no more than two huts of the same color.

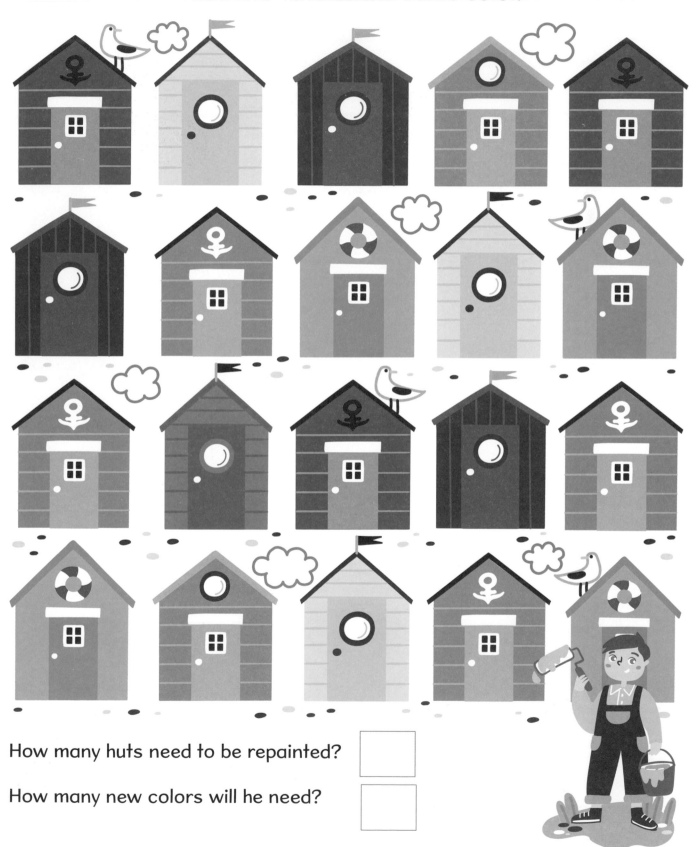

How many huts need to be repainted? ☐

How many new colors will he need? ☐

Magic Umbrellas
The pink and blue umbrellas are
magic and can change color!

How many magic umbrellas need to turn yellow
so there is an equal number of each color?

Blue [   ]   Pink [   ]

Missing Pictures

Copying one of the pictures at the bottom of the page, draw the missing pictures in each row.

Ducks in a Row

Circle the duck that comes next
in each line of ducks.

Which duck comes next?

Sock It to Me!

One of these socks on the clothesline is missing its pair. Can you find it, and figure out who owns it?

Sarah likes socks with spots.

Spencer loves striped socks. He also likes green.

Ben likes any sock that has some red.

Abby hates striped socks.

Flo likes any kind of sock, except green.

The odd sock belongs to:

Don't Burst My Balloon!

Draw a line to help the balloon through the maze without popping!

Fly a Kite!

Everyone in the park has a different kite, except Laura and Lulu. Circle their kites.

Lulu's brother has a kite too. The design on his kite starts with the letter "l" and ends with "g". Which is it?

Next Gnome

Circle the gnome that comes next in each line.

Which gnome comes next?

or

or

or

or

Bake Off!

These bakers can't agree about the shape of the cookies they are baking! Who will have the last word to decide the shape of the cookies?

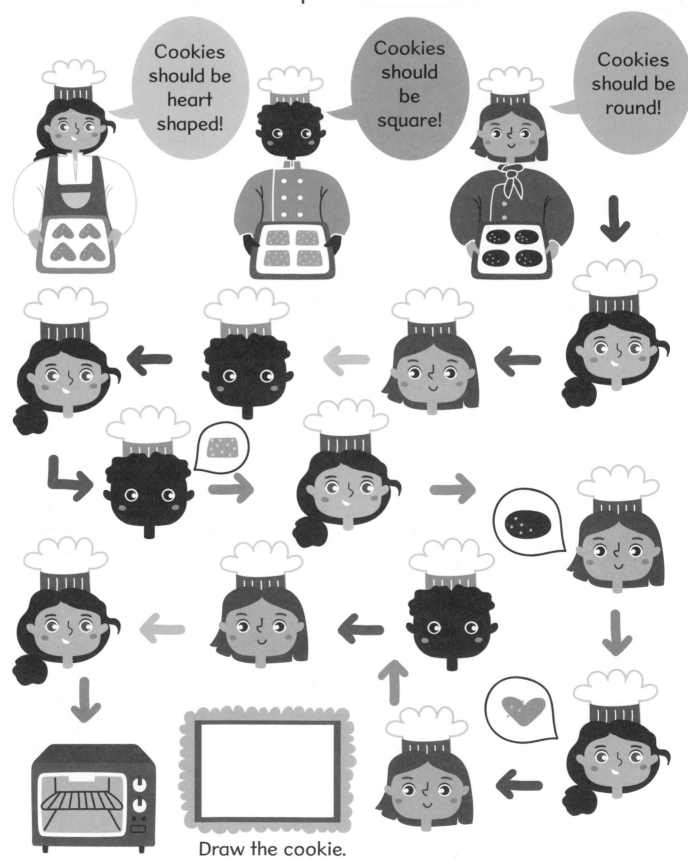

Draw the cookie.

Spot the Sheep

The farmer painted spirals on the sides of her sheep to mark that they belonged to her.

Spot, the sheepdog, is color blind and can only see red and blue! He rounds up the sheep with the colors he can see and forgets the rest. Circle the ones he forgets.

Elevator Logic

These people are all going to a party in the basement. The elevator only takes six people at a time. How many trips does the elevator need to make?

FLOOR 2 ⬍

FLOOR 1 ⬍

GROUND ⬍

The elevator makes this many trips:

BASEMENT ▲

Penguin Pals

Penguins need to stay together to keep warm.
The more in a group, the better.

These four lost penguins join either Penguin Pete's group or Penguin Pat's.

Penguin Pat

Penguin Pete

Three of the lost penguins join Penguin Pete's gang and one joins Penguin Pat's. Then two of Penguin Pat's group waddle off to the sea! How many are left in each group?

Penguin Pete's group:

Penguin Pat's group:

Curious Crab

There are four shapes at the bottom of the page that don't belong in the crab shape. Draw circles around the shapes.

TIP: Use colored pencils or felt-tip pens to fill in the shapes.

HINT: All of the colors are facing the right way.

Super Sandcastle

There are three shapes that don't belong in this sandcastle.
Which are they? Circle them.

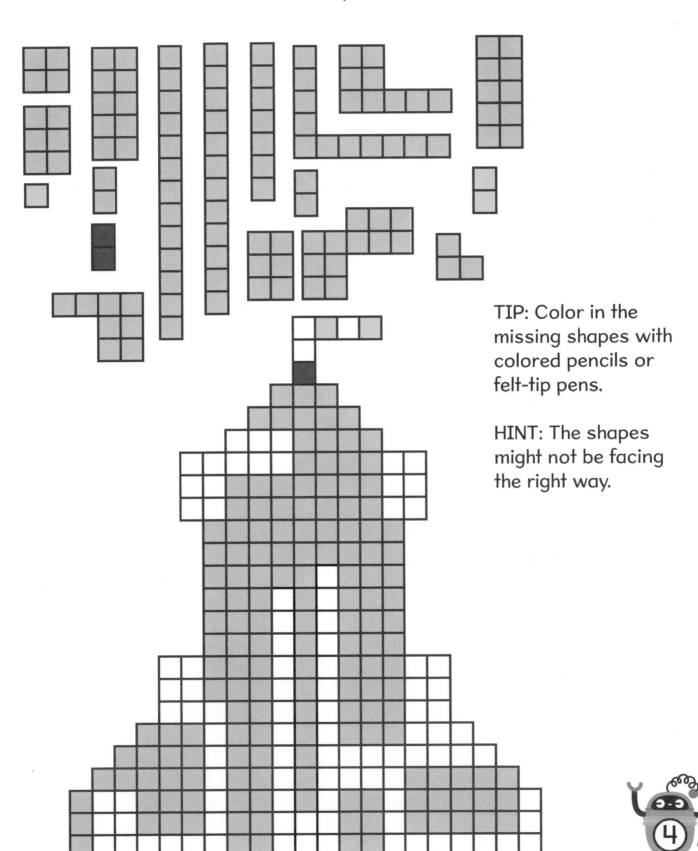

TIP: Color in the missing shapes with colored pencils or felt-tip pens.

HINT: The shapes might not be facing the right way.

4

Shape Sudoku

Draw the shapes in the grid so that there is only one of each shape in each row and column. The first row is done for you.

Shape Sudoku

Draw the shapes in the grid so that there is only one of each shape in each row and column. The first row is done for you.

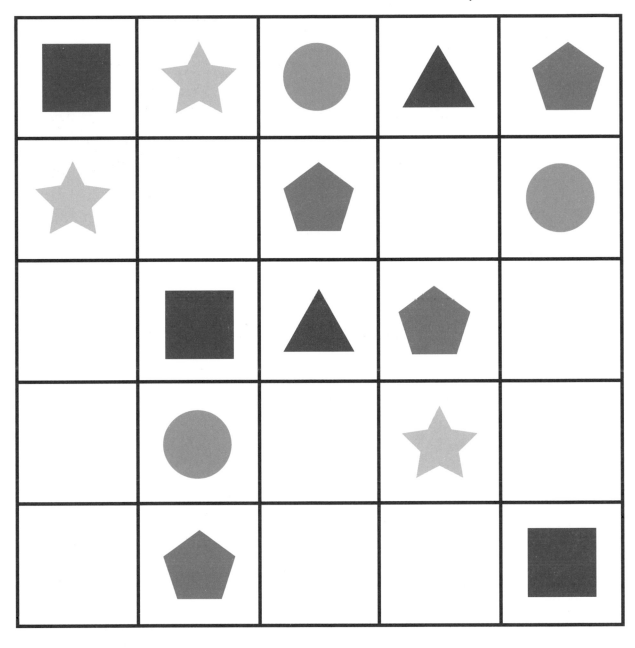

Fill the Space

Arrange these shapes to fit the grid. Use colored pencils or felt-tip pens to fill in the grid. Tip: Start in the top right-hand corner with a yellow pencil.

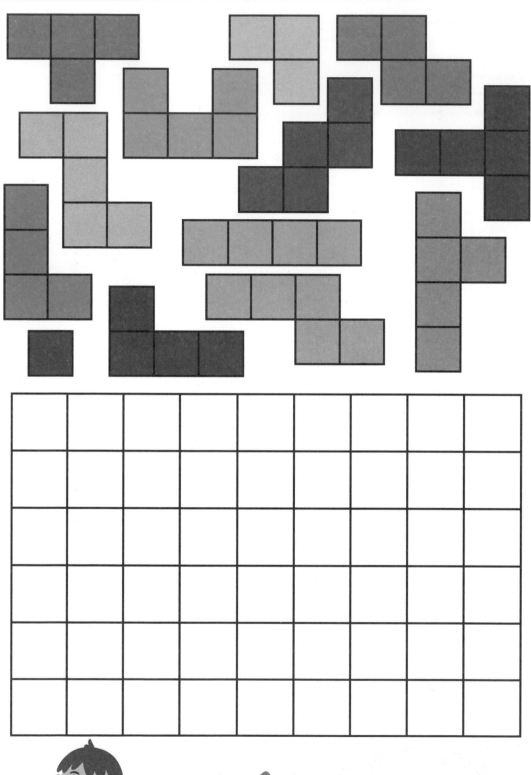

Catch a Cat

Help this dog through the maze to catch a cat!

15

Flock flying east

Hedgehog

E

1, 3, 2, 4

C & F

Ellie and George

C & H

Rachel

Right leg and
left arm

Sneakers

Fierce dinos, No

3

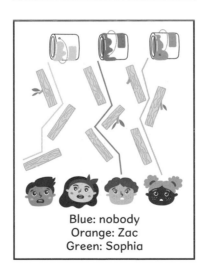

Prince Frederick's

Blue: nobody
Orange: Zac
Green: Sophia

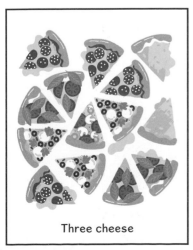

Three cheese

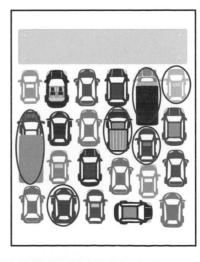

Henry: Bus
Jamie: Skateboard
Grace: Roller skates
Stephanie: Bike

18 people, 5 suitcases

A, C, E

Monday

Take the rabbit over, return; take the carrots over, return with the rabbit; take the fox over, return; take the rabbit over the river.

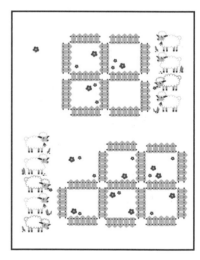

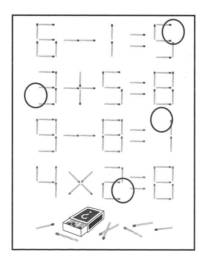

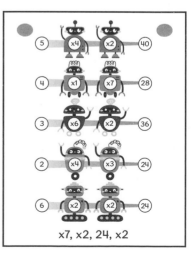

x7, x2, 24, x2

Amy   Harry   Jack

Sienna   Abeo   Sophie

7, 3

Blue: 1, Pink: 1

Spencer

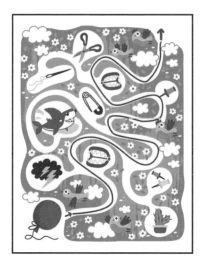

The ladybug kite

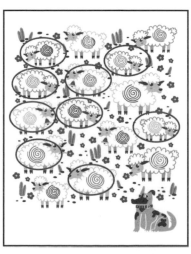

3

Pete's: 9, Pat's: 8

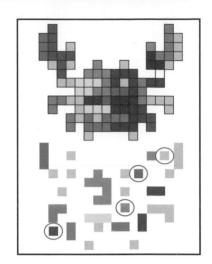

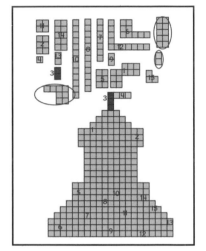

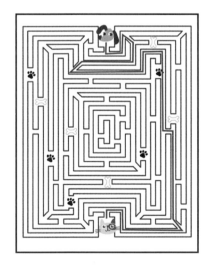